The Varmits

Dave Lamb

Illustrated by
John Lamb & Dave Lamb

Varmit House

Dedicated to my brother Dave, who made the world a better place through his humor and creativity.

To my grandson Elvis, whose love for The Varmits helped me see it was time to give Dave's story a new life.

Special Thanks to:

Rex, who led the way for our family when we needed it most.
Gary, whose musical talent and humor continues to inspire me.
Jack, for your vision and help in seeing this book through.
Moira, for the many reviews and edits.
Sheila Morris, for your guidance and counsel.
Paula, for your unwavering support.

Garrett, Katheryne, Austin, Mary, Gabby, and of course Elvis, I love you.

Varmits...

Varmits

live in every town.

Every now and then,
one comes around.

Everybody hides if
there's one in sight,

because varmits are children
who are not polite.

They can be short, tall,
big or skinny.

When it comes to manners,
they don't have any.

DUH
HI NEIGHBOR!
Ribbit
If you see a varmit
he won't say "Hi."

GOODBYE NEIGHBOR!
DUH
Ribbit
Ribbit
and when you walk away
he won't say "Goodbye."

She won't say "Thank You" and hates to say "Please".

SNEEZE

She won't cover her mouth
when she starts to sneeze.

He slams the door so hard
it could fall off the wall,

and sometimes he won't
even close it at all.

Dinner time finds her very rude.
Her arms are on the table

or her hands are in her food.

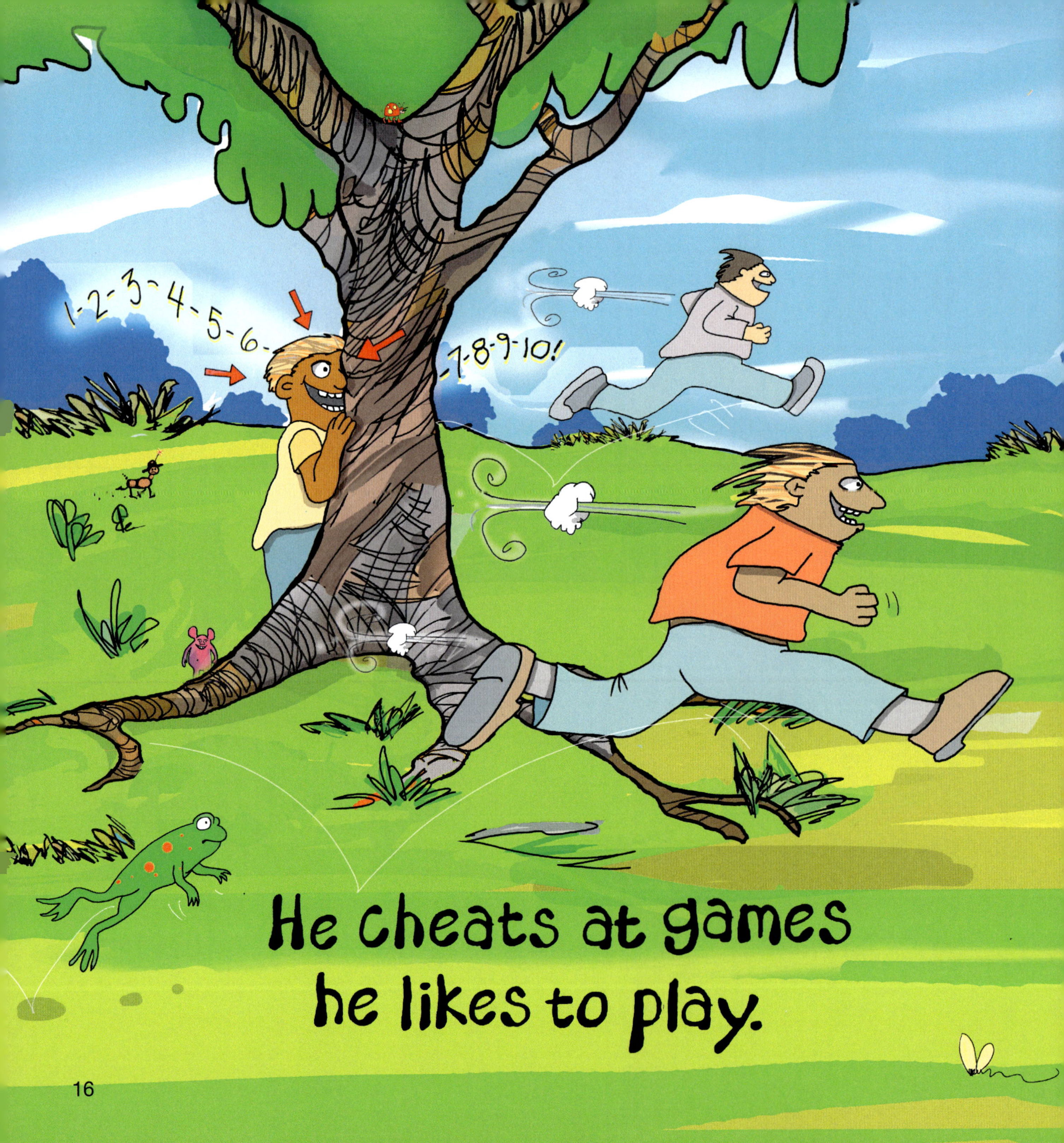

He cheats at games
he likes to play.

Though he knows the rules,
he will cheat anyway.

She will always try to take cuts in line,

and you will never see
her obeying a sign.

You can't play with his toys because he hates to share.

But if he can't play with yours,
he thinks it's not fair.

RAT
RAT
RAT
RAT

BLEAH!

WOW! VARMITS DON'T GET ALONG VERY WELL!

By reading this story it's not hard to tell,
that varmits do not get along very well.

It is also very easy to see, that a Varmit is someone you would not want to be.

If people don't like you,
they may run and hide.

then you really won't feel
very happy inside.

If you watch your manners
in everything you do,

you will like yourself better
when the day is through.

If you are kind
and treat others like a friend

WOW! WHAT A COOL TOY!
LOOK AT THOSE DUCKIES GO!
there's a good chance they
will want to play again.

When you ask with a please
and offer to share,

you will make pals
almost anywhere!

YOU'RE MY BEST PAL!
YOU'RE MY BEST PAL TOO!
When you are polite,
it's a very sure sign

I SURE LIKE HAVING A FRIEND LIKE YOU TO PLAY WITH!
ME TOO!
Ribbit
that people will be proud to say
"You're a friend of mine!"

About the Author & Illustrator

Dave Lamb was born in 1952. At an early age, he showed a talent for drawing, painting, and all things related to the creative arts.

In his teens, he wrote and illustrated three children's books. The Varmits was his last. Sadly, Dave passed away at age 18 before his illustrations for The Varmits were complete.

Dave's identical twin, John, has now completed The Varmits in the unique style that Dave and John created together.

About the Co-Illustrator

Among his many roles in life, father, artist, author and animator, John Lamb is now a grandfather and remains a working artist.

As identical twins, John and Dave collaborated on all their projects. Raised in a family of scrapbookers, John carefully kept all of Dave's work. Recently, John shared the original black and white copy of The Varmits with his grandson, Elvis.

Seeing Elvis' love for The Varmits, John realized it was time to finish Dave's work. This full color book is for Elvis, and you.

John won an Academy Award® in 1979 and an Emmy® in 2024 for achievements in Technology and Engineering.

Original Illustrations by Dave Lamb

The Varmits' Secret Search

- There is a lady bug on every page. Can you find it?
- Who do you think is the lady bug's best friend?
- How do the animals and insects respond when the children act like varmits?
- Do the animals and insects look happy when the children are happy?
- Who is your favorite character in the story?
- What is the frog trying to catch?
- Does the frog ever catch the fly?
- If you had a friend who acted like a varmit, what would you do?
- Who do you think has more fun? Varmits? Or children who are kind, share and have manners?

First Printing

ISBN 9798218437695

Varmit HOUSE

Made in the USA
Middletown, DE
19 January 2025